CW0085358.3

I HOPE THIS MAKES YOU FEEL
LESS ALONE

I HOPE THIS MAKES YOU FEEL
LESS ALONE

JORDIN WEST

To order additional copies of this book, contact:
Xlibris
1-888-795-4274
www.Xlibris.com
Orders@Xlibris.com
816226

CONTENTS

SORROW AND PAIN

HOPE BEYOND WHAT'S SEEN

ACKNOWLEDGEMENTS

Mahi for always believing in me.

Daddio for always investing in me.

Raymond for supporting me.

Cody for joy unlike any other.

Grandma and PePaw for grounding and strengthening me.

Ellie for always encouraging and helping me.

Alyssa for always reminding me.

And to the others who have helped make me who I am.

All who have loved me through it all.

TO YOU

To the mother who lost her child,

To the one struggling with addiction,

To the son who was abandoned,

To the veteran seemingly forgotten,

To the girl that was made an orphan by a car crash,

To the parent that feels like a failure,

To the daughter whose dad is emotionally unavailable,

To the black boy being treated in a disgusting manner,

To the girl who was raped,

To the parent watching their child make choices that break your heart,

To the man who is defined by his worst mistake,

To the boy who was assaulted but is too embarrassed to tell,

To the member of the LGBTQ+ community receiving hate from the church,

To the girl who took another's life while driving under the influence,

To the single-parent working three jobs in hopes of making ends meet,

To the child that is lost within the foster care system,

To the girl who carves hate-filled words into her skin,

To the man on death row who feels as though he threw his life away and hates himself for it,

To the immigrant who can't make it across the border,

To the woman who cannot forgive herself for having the abortion,

To the refugees running in sheer terror from the civil war in their home,

To the friend who carries deep regret for not recognizing the signs in the friend who took their life,

To the kids walking through life with a divided house, or two houses, and no place that feels like home,

To the husband who feels worthless and void of purpose because he isn't making enough to provide for his family,

To the one whose family was murdered,

To the girl who has been labeled a slut for making a singular mistake,

To the cop that walks around with fear weighing down on his shoulders and hopes to see his family for another night,

To the young black man that walks around with terror weighing down on his shoulders and hopes to see his family for another night,

To the granddaughter who lost her beloved grandmother,

To the one who feels they need to drink in order to make it through the day,

To the wife who feels stuck after losing the love of her life of over fifty years,

To the man who lost his family to his job,

To the one who has been hurt by the ones who were meant to make them feel safe,

To the lost, to the hurting, to the broken. . .

To *you.*

Whatever it is you are walking through, whatever pain, whatever loss, whatever description you relate to…

You are seen. Your pain is valid.

Nothing makes what you've experienced right, and I'm sorry.

But I can promise that you are not alone, and you *never* will be.

SORROW
AND PAIN

STUCK

I'm stuck here living a life that I don't want to live, but this seems to be all that there is.

LOST

Once was found, but now I'm lost.

DARKNESS

In the darkness, one of two things tend to happen.
You either find someone in it, or lose others in it.

TATTOOS

The scars run deep within
this tattooed body.

TIME-BOMB

Why am I like this? How can this be?

I push people away until they leave so that I can prove myself right as I believe that people always leave.

I truly think that I'm saving others from the explosion that is bound to take place.

I need people to run away and gain as much space so I don't blow up in their face and take away things that cannot be replaced.

I can no longer allow people to be taken hostage and be wounded in the midst of this battle I'm fighting against myself.

I don't want to cause others pain due to my own and the pride that refuses to let me ask for help.

So away from me, please…just go.

I will harm you otherwise, this I know.

I promise that this is better for you, though.

Save yourself and go.

For I'm a ticking time-bomb about to explode.

HOLD ON TO ME

Hold on to me because my hands are growing weak.
Not sure how much longer I'm able to just simply be.
Lord, won't You please come near to me?

LET ME BE

Just let me be sad.
Stop trying to force a smile onto my face.
Don't make me quickly move past the bad.
Please let me be, just extend me some grace.

HOSTAGE

I am a hostage to my own pride.
The lie that I can only be strong is one
      which I live by.
My pride is too real.
I can't ask for help, so I'll probably
      never heal.

BRAIN IS INSANE

I have this brain that drives me insane.
I fear some days that I can't withstand the pain.
I find my thoughts too difficult to explain.
I'm scared this way things will always remain.

HOW

How am I expected to keep breathing
when the air has abandoned my lungs?
How am I supposed to be happy
when nothing I do seems to be enough?
How come everyone leaves
if I'm "worthy of love?"
Am I allowed to be weak and not always have to be tough?

IDK

I've been someone that I don't know.
I've gone places that I shouldn't go.
I'll continue smiling, just putting on this show.
I'll do whatever I can to ensure that others can grow.

LACK OF FAITH

Is my lack of healing due to a lack of faith?
If I simply believed more, would I be healed?

SHIPWRECK, PART 1

(INSPIRED BY JONATHAN MARTIN)

The origin of this shipwreck doesn't really matter.

What matters now is simply the reality that you are drowning.

What matters now is the fact that the world you knew and loved is no longer the world you're in.

Philosophy won't help you down here.

Theology won't help you down here.

Platitudes won't help you down here.

That which you believe about shipwrecks and drowning doesn't cause those things to cease.

Religion won't do you much good down here.

Principles are incapable of keeping you warm as you descend into the depths, thousands of leagues below the surface.

There is not a single thing that can be found within a book or within a sermon or within a conversation that is able to overwhelm the facts of what you're experiencing.

All you can see is the endless dim of the bitter, subzero ocean.

You taste the reality in the saltiness of the water that you incidentally continue inhaling.

You feel the reality in the burning of the tears from your eyes.

It is within this experience that a hard truth hits you, one that you're unable to deny.

There is no returning to the life you once had…not anymore.

For the life you once had is no more.

DOUBT

I'm sorry all of your kindness
toward me has been repaid
with doubt.

ACTRESS

It takes so much courage to be honest about one's pain.
It takes such strength to allow oneself to be known.
It requires bravery to be vulnerable, to be open.
That may be courage that I simply don't possess.

"To be known is the only way to be truly loved."
I guess I'll never truly be loved because I just can't trust.
They say, "It's OK to not be OK."
If I allow myself to not be OK, they will always leave.

It's hard to be vulnerable.
It's easier to be an actress.
I can't love because it means I'd have to show them what's behind this mask.
I guess I settle for surface-level acquaintances because I won't let them in.

How can I be surprised when I'm left alone?
People want deeper friendships that I cannot offer.
I guess I just need greater courage, strength, and bravery.
That way I can finally let myself be truly seen.

CAN YOU LOVE A MASK?

People say that they love one another, I'm not sure that is true.

People don't actually know one another.

You can't know someone when all you see is the mask which they wear.

It's easy to 'love' someone when you only see them as they wish you to see.

Love is shown pure and is forged through the fire of trials.

You cannot love someone you fail to know.

Just as they can't love the person that you pretend to be.

They can't love your mask, just as you can't love theirs.

Will we ever have the courage to take off the masks?

Only then can we be truly known and truly loved.

TWENTY-ONE

Turned 21 today, I'm not sure how I feel.

Another year closer to death.

Another year further from innocence.

They celebrate me, but the celebration is incomplete.

It's hard to be happy when you're no longer here with me.

SHIPWRECK, PART 2

(JONATHAN MARTIN, THANK YOU AGAIN)

The way I see, everybody gets a tragedy.

Let me put it more poetically: everybody gets a shipwreck.

If you spend enough time on the water, something is bound to unfold in an unplanned manner.

Shipwrecks are serious, but they are also to be expected.

It's an inevitability.

The important thing is our response to the wreckage (diagnosis, loss, pain, etc.).

I mostly know about this from doing it improperly.

We all have differing ways in which we best learn.

Mine, apparently, is making massive misjudgments that lead to massive regrets. I then put a pen to a page in hopes that others will be able to avoid what I crashed head on with.

My first shipwreck: you could see me clinging to the mast, pretending that the ship would not go down simply due to the sheer force of my strength and will…DENIAL.

A later time, another shipwreck: I blamed everyone within any sort of distance…BLAME.

Yet another time: I allowed my relationship with God to become detached and routine. I allowed my anger to affect my view on absolutely everything, including but not limited to God's goodness, comforting, and ability to heal my heart...ISOLATION.

In the midst of a shipwreck, all of our instincts encourgae us to run for cover and to hide.

There is no healing within this response.

May we look the wreckage in the face.

May we look at both the light and dark within our own selves, and let the wreckage lead to intimacy between ourselves and God rather than distance.

The way I see it is, everyone gets a shipwreck.

How will you respond?

ANOTHER ONE

Another diagnosis placed
upon someone I love.
My heart grows heavier.
Please don't leave me too.
Please don't take them away.

CEMENT

I want to move forward.
I want to get past my hurts.
I want to get past my past.
But it seems that my feet are cemented to the ground.
I can't move.

HELPLESS

"What is it that causes you to feel helpless?" you asked me.
My reply was simple and concise.
"Death."

SO THEY SAY

People say that they respect vulnerability.
They say that they respect when one opens up.
Yet when I do that, I learn who I truly am
simply isn't enough.

HOW?

How is this world still spinning
when you're no longer in it?

HURT

I've hurt many people many times in my life...
But I've hurt myself the most.

TWENTY-FOUR, PART 1

Twenty-four hours can change everything.

From life to death.

From color to black.

From light to darkness.

From hope to loss.

HELL

You love me and you'd follow me to Hell. . .
I just am not willing to lead you there.
Leave. Please.

SAVING

I am incompetent of saving those
that I love, and I am trying to be
OK with that.
I'm not sure that I ever will be.

BANDAGE

I'm sorry.
You can't fix the scar you gave me
by covering it with a Band-Aid.

GUARDED

I never thought it a bad thing to put up my guard.

I was only doing it in order to keep myself and everyone else safe.

I guess I let the walls be built too high to climb.

I just can't be hurt again.

So guarded I will remain.

ESCAPEE

I escaped death plenty of times.
Still, something deep within me died along the way.

BEAR

The tears poured down her face as
she held every ounce of pain and
disappointment back.
Within her she held more than anyone
could possibly bear to know, let alone carry.

NO BEAUTY

There is no beauty in my
brokenness and sadness.
Do not romanticize this.

I MISS YOU

Such immense pain, to where do I go?
This weight that I'm bearing is too heavy.
What am I feeling? It's sorrow upon sorrow.
In this state, I can't measure up to all that I'm expected to be.
After so much time, I'm just expected to be fine.
Nobody checks in anymore. No one asks how I've been.
So the weight that I'm carrying seems to be solely mine.
It's as though the pain and loss has just been forgotten.
How nice it must be to be able to forget.
To not dwell on the pain and not drown in the sorrow.
I cannot force the thoughts out, it's become my permanent mind-set.
It hurts so much that oftentimes, I'm not sure that I'll make it to tomorrow.
"You know where she is, she's in a better place!"
"You need to grieve with hope, it will all be OK!"
That makes me feel no better as she's gone without a trace.
People don't understand that my whole world has turned to gray.
I'm told that time heals all wounds, I don't think that is true.
How can you heal the void of someone being taken away?
I know God is Healer, but I haven't seen healing come through.
The pain that I'm feeling is leading me astray.

I'm supposed to hold my tongue and say that I'm OK without you here.

What's done is already done.

I just feel unprotected without you near.

But I can't say that I'm OK. I'm really not.

I hope to see better days.

This gaping hole in my chest just hurts a whole lot.

It's been so hard since you were taken away.

I want you back with me, but I know that is just selfish.

Right now, God is holding you. Man, am I jealous.

NUMB

When becoming numb is the only way
for us to survive, we crave to feel alive.
But when we truly feel, we drown in
everything that went unfelt for so long.
And just like that, the fear switches it
all off yet again, believing it's safer.

WHEN?

When did my heart become so weak?
When did the light in my eyes fade?
When did I disappear into the darkness?
When did I start believing that I was nothing?
When did I forget that shined from my soul?
When did I begin seeing myself through the lens of these lies?

LOSS

Loss after loss, death after death.

It's as though someone is gone each time I take a breath.

So here I sit, struggling to hold the air in.

For I fear if I let it out, death with steal again.

Everyone that I love has been taken away.

I walk with dread to see who I will lose next, any given day.

My heart has broken over and over and over.

Every loss seems to cause time to move slower.

How do I process when I am given no break?

When will, from this nightmare, I wake?

It feels like I'm drowning, on my head crashes wave after wave.

I try to be so strong, but I'm truly about to cave.

I can't take another loss, I cannot lose another person.

I can't carry this horrible weight. Why have I been given this burden?

Am I bound to lose everyone that I care about?

I'm in such pain. There's simply no way out.

I'm scared to care because I'm scared they'll die.

I know I shouldn't, but I have to ask why.

I'm told that no one should be alone.

But everyone that I love is quickly taken, so I'm better on my own.

I don't know how to be OK.

Most times I fear that I won't even make it through the day.

How do I go on as if everything isn't all messed up?

When will enough be enough?

God… I cannot lose someone else. I can't.

Please, just a break would You grant?

My heart can't go through this anymore.

I know Life ultimately wins, but death seems to be winning this war.

My heart is shattered.

Why must I lose everyone that matters?

I hate that death is the most consistent thing in my life, apart from You.

Sometimes death just seems more real to me than You do.

Please don't leave me… just help me get through.

I just know I can't take losing You too.

TRAUMA

It causes us to break ourselves
down to fragments in order to survive.
We aren't left with any semblance
of self or of confidence.
It's the utter loss of ourselves
for a life that we never asked for.
What trauma doesn't teach you is
how to reconstruct yourself in order to survive.

LIFE OR DEATH (INSPIRED BY C. S. LEWIS)

You never know how much you truly
believe something until its truth or
falsehood becomes life or death to you.
Until holding on to the promises that
were spoken faces the death of a loved one.
Until having hope faces yet another diagnosis.
Until the faith you claimed faces your
greatest fears.
Until peace faces utter chaos.
Until light faces overwhelming darkness.
Until you must trust the rope to not only
hold that box but now trust it to be capable
of bearing your weight over the edge.
Did I ever truly believe if my faith is so
shaken within this storm?
If my house is swiftly knocked over with one
gust of the wind, my house was likely only a
house of cards to begin with.

It was never capable of surviving this storm to begin with.
What authority do I have to doubt all of the
things that I once boldly proclaimed?
What is it that we can do with suffering,
except suffer it?

WITHIN

There's something deep within
me that lives only to destroy me.
And if it's incapable of ripping me
apart, it seeks to do so to someone
that I love.
I hate this part of me.

LOST MORE

My life has been a constant theme of loss.

Loss of hope, loss of innocence, loss of those I love.

I'm twenty-one years old and I've lost many people I love.

I'm twenty-one years old and I lost my innocence years ago.

I'm twenty-one years old and I've lost hope more times than I can count.

How does one lose so much in so little time?

How is one to continue in joy when all that's been known is sorrow?

How can one not fall into the fear telling her that every single person she loves will be taken sooner rather than later?

How does one not begin to blame oneself, recognizing every mistake with each precious loss?

FOG

Loss is overwhelming, it seems to be my only constant.
(I know God is constant, just hard to see sometimes. Death is always easily seen.)
My heart is heavy.
Grief is a fog that I cannot see through.
Won't You just come near?

ALL TOO WELL (I LOVE TAYLOR SWIFT)

Death… known all too well.

My life was together, but then apart it fell.

You came as a thief in the night.

You took all that I have, and that's not alright.

You came unexpected and uninvited.

You left me here questioning what it is I did.

What did I do so wrong?

How does everyone still expect me to be strong?

I've lost more people than the years I've lived.

You took advantage of me, took more than I can give.

All those I love seem to be lost.

Is love worth all that it costs?

Each death creates an even bigger hole in my heart.

One more light goes out, and I'm lost in the dark.

Each of them takes a piece of me…

There's no way that I can be all you want me to be when I'm incomplete.

Why did You take them? Why'd they have to leave?

It cannot be for my good… that I can't believe.

"It's no good for man to be alone," so You say.

If that's the case, why would you take them all away?

They say that all that is done is for our good and Your glory.

All that's been done simply fills me with fury.

I'm mad at You for taking them.

Is it because it's me that You condemn?

Is it because I've messed up so much?

Do I no longer deserve to be around great people as such?

Now I don't know what to say.

The pain won't go away.

I've been crying since that day,

When you took my good away.

Here, alone, God has forced me to stay.

I'm not sure I'll ever again be able to say I'm OK.

I'M SORRY

I look into the eyes that have cried many tears for all the lies and pain buried inside.

The only word he speaks is, "Why?"

I wish there was an answer I could supply, but I don't want to lie.

It's that cut-and-dry.

He asks, "How am I expected to get by? I simply want to die and finally defy all that is eating me alive."

I didn't want to pry but I knew I had to try.

He said that everything had gone awry as he let out a deep sigh that he must have been holding within all night.

I tried to encourage him that it would all be all right and to keep up the fight until all of these wrongs were made right and justified.

He couldn't find an end in sight, and he could only feel his fright. There was no longer delight, at least not on this night.

I should have been physically present to hold him tight and be a bright light despite the joy he seemed to have been denied.

I have regrets. Within I have a divide because I didn't do enough and my friend died that night.

Now I also only have one word to speak: "Why?"

I look into the mirror, at my eyes that have cried many tears for the loss on the darkest night and the pain I have buried deep inside.

QUESTIONS

Tears running down my face and I yell, there's no one to tell.
I was completely alone as to the ground I fell.
How do You want me healed? Yet I'm still not well.
How about You take my pain and send it to Hell?
Until You do, I'll be locked in this cell.
I'm no longer a person, only an empty shell.
Will that not be the case if in You I dwell?
People encourage me to cry out to You.
To be honest, it's the last thing I want to do.
Do You even see what I'm going through?
After all I've done, You can't possibly make me new.
I feel You so distant as I sit in this pew.
Why won't You just break through?
Break through my stubbornness, break through my hurt.
Break through the grime, break through the dirt.
Won't You, once again, remind me of my worth?
Why is nothing coming out of all that I exert?
Why is my mind the breeding ground for fear?
Why can't I understand when it's Your voice I want to hear?
I hold it all together as I catch my falling tear.
You're on Your throne. Why won't You just come near?

You are to me as water is to a deer.

Yet You still don't seem to come and meet me here.

Here in my pain, here in my loss.

They say, "You know He loves you, just look at the cross."

How am I to believe that when to the side I'm tossed?

If I've truly been found, how can I be so lost?

I'm trapped in the darkest night.

I'm here without sight.

Why is it so dark when they say that You're light?

I'm in the midst of the hardest fight of my life.

As time passes, it's harder to believe it will be all right.

Every time the fear comes, my chest feels tight.

I try to fight it with all of my might.

I sit here paralyzed, just waiting for daylight.

But it never seems to come.

What's worse? To feel it all or to be numb?

Look to the heavens for where does my help come from?

I keep looking up…

But help never seems to come.

ANOTHER LIGHT, PART 1

Another light goes out. . .

There's so much pain, but who cares?

There are still so many lights left in the world.

I know that I should just be thankful for the memories and time I did have.

I KNOW.

But that brings me no comfort, no hope, no peace.

Just pain.

People minimize the process of grief and think that it should fit nicely into this box:

It should last this long, in this manner, with these people, in this way, then you'll be fine.

But what about when the grief process doesn't fit into this box that has been created?

What do you say to those people then?

To the people that don't have a quick get-happy plan to get through the grief and be OK again?

To the people that are constantly followed by the haunting memories?

To the people that had to watch the life leave the eyes of someone that they love dearly?

To the people drowning under the waves of grief?

To the people that see no way through the darkness?

To the people like me?

Is there anything to say?

What right do you have to tell another what their process of surviving should look like?

ANOTHER LIGHT, PART 2

Another light goes out in the sky of my love.

Now I stumble in an even darker darkness, which I didn't think was possible.

Don't judge someone else's process of getting through a hopeless situation.

Just be a light that they need and be present.

No one should walk through the dark...

Especially not alone.

HOPE BEYOND
WHAT'S SEEN

CLAY

The clay need not speak.

ABSOLUTE

Truth is absolute.
You can bend it.
You can spin it.
You can shade it.
You can deny it.
Yet absolute it remains.

LOCK

I lock into perfect hope today.

PERSPECTIVES (EVAN, THANK YOU)

There are billions of perspectives.
There's only a singular truth.

LET IT BE

Chains be broken.
Eyes be opened.
Hearts keep hoping.
Minds keep knowing.
His goodness keeps showing.
Hope is something that never stops flowing.

REDEEMER

Can I really get back what has been stolen?

They say You're a Redeemer. Does that mean You can fix what's broken?

GET LOST

The best part about being a human
is the ability to get lost.
It is when we are lost in the
wilderness that we find the depths
of who we truly are.

SPEAK

People who feel weak
become empowered
as you speak.
So speak.
Your voice matters.

DESTINY

The destiny you see for yourself
is way too small.
You are intended to do things
for His glory and for the betterment
of those around you.

CHANGE

"When the pain of change is greater than the pain of staying the same, then you'll change."
Don't wait that long.

CARRIES

Her vulnerability carries freedom.

Her voice carries truth.

Her heart carries hope.

Her mind carries wisdom.

Her body carries grace.

Her being carries holiness through the Spirit.

SAVIOR

You can never be too weak for a Savior. . .
But you can be too strong.

PRESENCE

His presence can calm any
storm you're going through.
His presence can comfort any
broken heart you encounter.
His presence can bring strength
to those who feel the weakest.
His presence can bring hope to
those within the most hopeless
situations.
His presence changes everything.

FORGIVENESS

I wish I would have known this a long time ago:
There is no weakness in forgiveness.
It actually shows great strength.
Forgive them, set yourself free.
Forgive yourself, become who you're created to be.

NO MORE STRIVING

You don't have to strive for acceptance. . .

You already have it.

Thrive from the acceptance which you already possess.

TWENTY-FOUR, PART 2

Twenty-Four hours can change everything.

From death to life.

From black to color.

From darkness to light.

From loss to hope.

KNOW

Daily know Him more until
we know Him fully.

IDENTITY

We can't know our purpose if
we don't first know our identity.

REMEMBER

I don't want to forget because of the pain;
I simply want to be able to remember without feeling it all over again.

FEELINGS ARE NOT TRUTH

Feeling like you're alone does not make you alone.

Feeling like a failure does not make you a failure.

Feeling like a burden does not make you a burden.

Feeling forgotten does not mean you are forgotten.

Feeling like you're not enough does not mean you are not enough.

Feeling like you're too far gone does not mean you are too far gone.

Feeling like you're dumb does not mean you are dumb.

Feeling like you're insignificant does not mean you are insignificant.

Feeling like you're unlovable does not make you unlovable.

Just because you feel something does not make it true.

Feelings do not equate to truth.

SHAME

You call my name, and
You silence my shame.

THERE YOU ARE

Where most people are most terrified to go,
there You are most powerfully manifested.

CHANGE

Any time that there is change,
there is loss.
That doesn't mean there can't be gain.

CAPTIVATED

We search for similarities in one
Another, and we end up missing
the opportunity to be captivated
by the beauty found within
our differences.
Diversity is central to the Body.
Diversity is beautiful.
Diversity is necessary.

LIGHT (HAITIAN PROVERB)

Men anpil, chay pa lou.
With many hands, the load
is made light.

TIPTOE NOT

Run, hop, skip, or dance to
wherever it is you're going.
Please just don't tiptoe there.

HOPE WHISPERS

As I sit lost and broken in the darkness,
Hope draws close to whisper in my ear:
"Do not give up."
"We are going to get there."
"It's not over."
"There is beauty, even here."

STRENGTH

My strength has been quite different these days.
It's no longer loud and boisterous.
It's quieter, closer to silent.
It's no longer hard and rigid.
It feels soft now.
It no longer wavers and is no longer unsure.
It holds steady, it is certain.
It's not as obvious any longer, but it's still there.
It's still there.

THERE'S GOOD PEOPLE

There's a lot of people that You've placed in my life.

People that I've continually pushed away.

I know that isn't right of me to do.

It's just due to fear that they'll walk away on their own someday.

But You've placed them here, and to this day, they refuse to move.

I don't understand, and I constantly ask why.

Every day, with consistency, they clearly reflect You.

They love me well and never stop trying.

How blessed I am to have them near.

They are always willing, for me, to fight.

No matter what, they say, "I'm here."

They never let me isolate and hide.

They see something in me that I fail to see within myself.

I wish to see myself through their eyes and Yours.

They see great potential, and they attempt to pull it out.

Open my eyes to see an identity that endures.

WORRY

A lot of people worry about me. . .
Of course, not any who truly know me.
Just the ones that think they do.
The ones who don't know what I've been through.
The ones who haven't stuck around long enough.
They'll never know this strength which I possess.

ENEMY'S LIES

The enemy will do all that he can
do to convince you that your gifts
are ordinary and your pain is unique.

You'll believe that your gifts are less
than and your pain is greater than.

And you'll feel alone, but don't buy those lies.

WHO TOLD YOU?

Who told you that your voice doesn't matter?
Who laughed at the thoughts and ideas that you shared after all the
courage you had to build up to speak?
I am here to tell you to not be quiet.
Be loud and be known.
Your voice matters. Your words have an impact.
You matter.
Do not let them silence your voice.

WEIRD

I've been consistently defined
as weird for a majority of my life.
It used to bother me.
That is, until I came to the
realization that my normal is
simply a whole lot more fun
and better than theirs.

KINDNESS

To be kind is completely free.
To be kind shows that love is still
available in a hurting world.

PLEASE

Please keep fighting.
Please keep waking up each morning.
Please keep your light shining.
Please keep hope because it gets better.
Please keep going because we need you to.
Please, we need you here.
Please, we WANT you here.

KEEP FIGHTING

Keep fighting.

Even when you don't feel like it, keep fighting.

Even when you don't want to wake up, keep fighting.

Even when you can't bear the weight of your body, keep fighting.

Even when you struggle to get out of bed, keep fighting.

Even when you can't hear anything but the lies, keep fighting.

Keep fighting because you are worthy of life and you are worthy of recovery.

Keep fighting.

LOVE FIRST

Love is the only thing that
is capable of changing people.
Let us love first.
Before judging.
Before condemning.
Before doubting.
Before thinking.
Before hating.
Love first.

NOTHING

You are not walking through all of this for nothing.
Something greater is in store for you.
You pain is not in vain.
Nothing is wasted.

TODAY

Don't let the storm from
yesterday cloud your skies today.
Focusing on the pain of yesterday
rather than the joy of today is
simply wasting another day.
Enjoy today.
Appreciate the small things.
Celebrate the small victories.

FOUND

As you are found in this moment,
you are loved and treasured.

WHAT I WANT

I just want to write and speak
things that actually mean
something to someone.

FREEDOM

Giving people the opportunity
and permission to misunderstand
you is where true freedom is found.

SILENCE

It's great to have encouraging
and thought-provoking things
to say.
But sometimes we just don't
have anything profound to say.
Silence is OK. Good even.

FIRE

I'm walking through the fire.
Fire can refine or destroy.
Fire can strengthen or devour.
I choose to be refined and to be strengthened.

MY LIFE

I want to spend the rest of
my life helping other people
feel less broken and unworthy
and more cherished and wanted.

LIGHT

Light is still light even if
it is dim, and you are still
loved even when you
don't feel like it.

LISTEN

Listen to their story without
trying to fix it.
That's where relief is found.

MORE

You are more than your worst
thoughts and your worst moments.

FAILURE

Failure is an event,
not an identity.

LEAVE

If people make you feel
as though you are hard
to love, leave.

HEALTHY

Happy does not equal healthy.

ENTER

I may not be able to fix what
you're going through, but I
am capable of entering into
your pain.
I can be with you in that hard
place.
You don't have to face anything alone.

INTERRUPT

Let us interrupt hatred.
Let us interrupt judgment.
Let us interrupt racism.
Let us interrupt violence.
Let us interrupt hypocrisy.
Let us interrupt misrepresentation.
Let us interrupt prejudice.
Let us interrupt injustice.

WAVES

During the storm, it's hard
to stay afloat in the waves.
I'm learning to be grateful
and learning to kiss the waves
for there is beauty even in
the pain.

JOY

Sometimes your heart can be sad while still having joy.
That's OK.

REACH

Preaching is awesome.
But it doesn't matter if
you're not reaching.

NO EXCUSE

How many people have I harmed simply
      because I was hurting at that current moment?
I used the phrase "hurt people hurt people" as
      an excuse for a while.
Then I came to the realization that being broken is
      no excuse for me to break someone else,
      whatsoever.
There is no justification for the pain purposefully
      placed on another due to the pain you personally
      are walking through.
There is no justification for hurting another because
      you are hurt yourself.
May we permit our wounds to cause us to become
      kinder and gentler, not crueler and more rigid.

HOPE

Hurting with hope still hurts.
It doesn't mean you're doing it wrong.

SPEAK

We become whoever the people
we love most say that we are.
May we speak kind words that edify.
May we speak loving words that promote change.
May we speak gentle words that lead to hope.
May we speak true words that lead to repentance.
May we speak words that better others and ourselves.

REJECTED

Your rejection is rejected
by complete acceptance.

SURVIVOR

I'm a survivor.

I will no longer define myself as a victim.

I am a warrior, a fighter, a survivor.

Since I have made it through all that I have, I can make it through anything.

I've survived so much and have only come out of it all stronger than before.

I am a survivor of abuse, hatred, anger, and death.

I am a fighter.

I'm no longer fighting against but fighting for.

Fighting for hope, for peace, for life, for love, for healing.

I may never reach it or obtain it in this life, but I'll fight nonetheless.

All I've ever known is the fight.

Now I guess I can embrace it as a part of my journey for growth.

I've never made it without a fight, and I doubt I ever will.

So fighting for what I deserve, I shall continue.

There is more.

I am a survivor.

MY HOPES

My hope is that in reading this,
you discovered hope in the
midst of your battle.
That you found another one
in the midst of the storm,
knowing you're not alone.
And that you can use these
words as reminders when
you need them.

LOVED

You are loved beyond comprehension.

NO LONGER

Let us no longer clean our hands while
neglecting to purify our hearts.
For our hands will act based off what is within.
So let's ask for renewed hearts that pursue
righteousness and justice.
Let's ask for changed hearts that recognize the value
others possess and treat them in the appropriate manner.
Let's ask for loving hearts that love before anything.

WITHOUT

I often wonder who I would be had my life
 lacked all of the pain I've experienced.
I feel as though I would be someone completely
 different altogether.
I would be weaker, crueler, apathetic, hateful, and lost.
Without my suffering, I don't believe I would have
 emerged with such great strength.
Without my loss, I don't believe I would be capable
 of valuing those around me.
Without my pain, I don't believe I would have learned
 to be kind and gentle towards others when they
 may be experiencing similar things.
Without my darkness, I don't believe I would have
 recognized and appreciated the light while
 I hold it.
Without my tragedies, I don't believe that I would
 be open about my emotions to trustworthy
 people surrounding me.

Without my scars, I don't believe others would be
    able to look at me and have hope of healing.
Without the fire I walked through, I don't believe I would
    possess a character that has been forged through
    the flames and is better for it.

WRESTLED

I wrestled with God, refusing
to let go until He blessed me,
until He revealed Himself to me.
I walked away from that fight and
I recognized that I now walk with
a limp.
This limp will always be a part of me,
will always be a reminder of Him.
The limp is simply a reminder of grace
and a visible reminder of my need.
I would never exchange this pain
and discomfort for anything.
I will forever walk with a limp, but
I am better for it.

SPECIAL MENTIONS

Joanie— thank you for honest conversations. You make me better.

Josh— thank you for immeasurable fun
and for being my chosen family!

Curtis (Papa Noel)— thank you for always
making me laugh and supporting me.

Alyson— thank you for the joy you carry
and bring to everyone around you.

Michelle— thank you for believing in me
and seeing greatness in me.

Lightning Source UK Ltd.
Milton Keynes UK
UKHW010312150920
369915UK00003B/66/J

9 781664 119567